The Way We Were

~ HAURAKI GULF ~

Text by
Kirsten Warner

HODDER MOA BECKETT

We thank the following people for allowing us to use their photographs. In many instances dates, locations and identities are unknown. We apologise for any photographs that have been attributed to the wrong geographical areas but hope you agree that they convey the mood of early New Zealand.

M. Anderson	G. Eagles	E. McHardie	L. Subritzky
L. Bailey	M. Elliot	Mercury Bay District Museum	J. Sweney
R.H. Bailey	Mr Ellis	G.K. Miller	A. Tetley
W. Beckett	J.N. Fairgray	R. Morath	R. Towers
I. Bedford	B. & L. Fletcher	J. Munk	C. Flinn
C. Bedggood	Mrs Flinn	N. Naden	J. Ward
D. Betterton	W. Gordon	C.H. Newton	J. Watson
L. Boyd	D. Gray	Z. Northmore	C. White
R. Bree	U.A. Griffiths	M. Philson	S.A. Wigglesworth
M. Buchanan	R.F. Harvey	G. Riethmaier	J.F. Wilkinson
D. Burns	J. & R. Mabbett	J.S. Say	S. Woodhead
Mrs Delugar	J. Mantell	L. Smith	
V. Dixon	M. Mason	V.J. Smytheman	
L. Dutton	C. McCathie	P. Stein	

ISBN 1-86958-149-0

© Hodder Moa Beckett Publishers Limited

Published in 1995 by Hodder Moa Beckett Publishers Limited
Member of the Hodder Headline Group.
PO Box 100-749, North Shore Mail Centre, Auckland 1330.

Designed and produced by Hot House Design Group Ltd.
Printed through Colorcraft Ltd, Hong Kong.

All rights reserved. No part of this publication may be reproduced (except brief passages for the purpose of a review), stored in a retrieval system or transmitted in any form or by any means, electronic, mechanical, photocopying, recording or otherwise, without the prior written permission of the publishers.

INTRODUCTION

The Way We Were

~ HAURAKI GULF ~

FROM OUR EARLIEST YEARS, NEW ZEALANDERS hear the chant of the weather forecaster on the radio warning of rising south-westerlies "from Bream Head to Cape Colville". To the racing yachtsman or homesick fisherman that phrase conjures up the many sights, smells and challenges of the islands and landfalls of the Hauraki Gulf, the spectacular marine pathway to New Zealand's largest city, Auckland.

The Gulf does not have fearful pirates or the extremes of weather of other stretches of ocean, but in its own way it is one of the most romantic, beautiful and challenging marine playgrounds in the country, and always has been. It is an expanse of water bordered by the Coromandel Peninsula, Great Barrier Island, the Mokohinaus and Hen and Chickens, and reaches as far north as Whangarei Heads and southeast to Cuvier Island.

Predominantly, the history of the islands of the Gulf is a boating history. For over 1000 years of human habitation, these marine pathways and channels have been constantly travelled, firstly by Maori canoe fleets of war or trade, then later by the sailing ships, yachts, scows, schooners, cruisers, freighters and steamships of European settlement. Shipping was the primary method of transport around the nation's first commercial capital, Auckland, and its estuaries, rivers and Gulf islands.

When Captain James Cook explored the coastline on the *Endeavour*, he found the greater concentrations of Maori population north from the Bay of Plenty to Northland. Auckland was well populated, and the Gulf islands provided safety for Maori settlements. Captain Cook did not go beyond the outer islands into the Waitemata Harbour. The first European to do so was missionary Samuel Marsden in the 1820s, although not long after that the French mariner Dumont D'Urville explored the inner Gulf, leaving his name on the D'Urville Rocks north of Waiheke Island.

These early visitors were quickly followed by sealers, whalers, then traders, missionaries and later settlers. There was some attempt at European settlement of the Gulf in the mid-1820s when Waiheke Island was bought from the Maori. But travelling war parties of Ngapuhi from the north

This was the way photos were taken until the thirties when hand-held cameras became easily available. Most of the remarkable pictures in this book before that date would have been taken using the slow and cumbersome tripod camera like this one – being photographed using another tripod camera.

struck fear into the hearts of isolated settlers and they moved on. Europeans, however, brought with them the ravages of disease, which proved even more deadly and decimated the Maori population of the Auckland region.

A year after the signing of the Treaty of Waitangi in 1840 the European capital had shifted south from the Bay of Islands to Auckland, and settlers bought or took up disused Maori land, purchasing large parts or all of the various islands of the Gulf, which were quickly settled.

The Gulf provided a wealth of resources for the growing town. Much of the early building was done with shingle shipped from Waiheke Island, which also ran a brisk trade in manuka firewood and charcoal. Mineral deposits were found and mined on Kawau and Waiheke Islands, and there was a short-lived gold rush on Great Barrier.

The rich fish life of the Gulf, which had always supported Maori populations, now supported settlers whose resources were limited to what they could eke out from the land and sea and buy from the infrequent visits of trading ships.

Albert Sanford, a seaman who jumped ship in 1864, first worked as shipbuilder in Devonport, then began fishing in the Hauraki Gulf. He lived and farmed at Rakino Island, building the Sanford's fishing empire alongside the successful Maori commercial fishermen of that time. The Gulf was fished as if the bounty of oysters, mussels, crayfish, snapper, flounder and other gill fish was an endless resource, and early photographs show the mammoth proportions of the catches.

The mighty kauri, which had grown for hundreds of years on every hill and gully of the region, including Waiheke, Great Barrier and other islands, provided the raw material for a timber boom. The huge, straight logs were shipped to England for spars for the British Navy, then milled and sawn for building timber for Auckland, Australia and further afield. A valuable by-product was the golden kauri gum.

Milling continued longer on Great Barrier Island than most places, only coming to a halt in the 1940s when the Kauri Timber Company finally closed its Whangaparapara operation. In its heyday, a bustling village of more than 300 people ran the mill, port and support services such as bakery, butchery and bullock transport.

Once the kauri was taken out, clearing for farm settlement began. The resort potential of the Gulf islands, in particular Waiheke, was recognised very early, and by the time the Northern Steamship Company was formed in 1881 the colonial passion for boating and picnic excursions was gathering momentum. The photographs in this book show only a fragment of the 50 glorious years of the steamers.

Stock being loaded onto the scow Rahiri from an inlet on Waiheke Island.

Literally thousands of picnickers packed the decks in their narrow-waisted long skirts and high-necked collars and ties, wearing hats and boots and in their Sunday best. On shore at places like Kawau Island, Home Bay on Motutapu Island (where a menagerie of exotic wildlife included zebras, emus and peacocks) and Cowes Bay on Waiheke Island, they engaged in greasy pig competitions and boat races, ate from spit roasts and strolled along the shores.

The first boarding houses started at the farmsteads at the bays, where the families put up tents, then built cabins and boarding wings for summer guests. These enterprises employed everyone in the big families of the day, running launches to and from Auckland and for fishing, cooking on massive wood stoves, preserving fruit from farm orchards, making butter, cheese and soap, washing acres of linen, growing vegetables and gathering seafood.

Although such accounts sound idyllic, hardship and isolation was the everyday reality for the early settler families. The mostly previously unpublished photographs in this book are largely from family albums, taken mainly at leisure and social gatherings, and do not really show the other side of life.

The Way We Were

Seaside style circa 1916. Hats, braces and rolled-up trou are the order of the day.

looms out from the haze like a Viking stronghold, with great fiords, safe harbours, rocky cliffs and wide, white sand beaches dividing the coastline.

Life on the islands relied on regular contact with the boating traffic of the Gulf to transport stock, supplies, produce, mail and passengers as well as provide contact with the outside world.

A guidance system of lighthouses, established early because of the perils of the coastline, starts to the north where most shipping has entered the Gulf since Europeans arrived in this country. From Bream Head the channel heads past the big light on Coppermine, down until the light on Flat Rock signals the approach of Little Barrier Island and welcomes boats into the rising loom of the great light on Tiritiri Matangi. The channel passes seaward of Tiri, then north of Rangitoto Island the harbour pilot boat darts out of Auckland to put customs officers aboard and guide ships into the harbour.

No matter where you went on the Gulf there was activity — small fishing dinghies, racing and cruising yachts, cabin cruisers, steam trawlers trailing flocks of seagulls, sand shags, the constant movement of shipping carrying the comforts of life and lubricating the wheels of industry, ferries carrying passengers for business and pleasure. This is the way we were on the Hauraki Gulf for well over 100 years.

Waiheke Island was subdivided for holiday homes from the first two decades of this century, but the population declined on Great Barrier Island as mining and milling came to an end. The land was in large part farmed, and communities were isolated by the rugged terrain and insular attitudes. The decline in coastal shipping after the war spelled the end of the farming boom on Great Barrier, and much of the grazing land reverted to scrub, the unproductive land only recently sold to lifestylers attracted by the mysterious beauty and remoteness of the Gulf's largest island. The island

~ HAURAKI GULF ~

From the Early Days to the '50s

The Way We Were

Ellen Callaghan Regan was the mother of the first known European child born at Waiheke Island in 1841. Ellen Regan was born in 1809 in County Cork in Ireland. She and her husband John emigrated to Australia, where only one of their five children survived. They continued on to New Zealand and settled at Huruhe or Man O'War Bay on the sheltered eastern side of the island, where John milled kauri for ships' masts.

Waiheke Island's first European child, Mary Regan, born on Christmas Day, 1841, at Man O'War Bay. She lived into her 101st year and was at one time the oldest European in New Zealand. Mary married Henry Parker in 1864 and had at least 12 children who continued their lives at Waiheke. When Mary was born, the bay was already the home of the island's first European resident, trader Thomas Maxwell, who married into the tribe controlling large areas of the Hauraki Gulf. In 1837 Maxwell bought 3000 acres, built several houses and a store and started milling.

Hauraki Gulf

Awaawaroa Bay, Waiheke Island, site of an early manganese mine. It was settled early and the Gordon family farmed there for over 100 years, also running the island's first telephone exchange, small store, post office and guesthouse, busy until the 1930s.
The Northern Steamship Company built a wharf in 1908. Despite their isolation, the Gordons maintained high standards of behaviour and dress, seen in this photograph taken before the turn of the century near where settler William Gordon built his second home in 1900.

The Way We Were

The Alcock home at Harataonga in 1895, with members of the large family sitting on a fallen log in the foreground. Pioneer William Alcock arrived on Great Barrier Island in the late 1860s to take up government land grants. The house was probably built in the 1880s. Rough fencing and stockades, newly cleared paddock and plain buildings illustrate the settlement of the farming region of Great Barrier.

Hauraki Gulf

For over 100 years, the islands of the Hauraki Gulf have been Auckland's marine playground, providing safe and easy day trips. In this photograph small sailing craft can be seen as well as big steamers whose passengers, in 1895, were attending the Oddfellows Society picnic at Home Bay, Motutapu ("Sacred Island"). A big picnic, so popular in the 1890s, with bands playing and barrels of beer, brought up to 5000 people to the bay. Two brothers called Reid bought the island in 1869 and their families owned it for 80 years. Their hospitality was famous and parties sailed from Auckland to shoot wallaby, red deer, emu and ostrich.

The Ryan house at Okupu on Great Barrier in the 1890s. Like many of the Great Barrier settlers, the reputedly hot-tempered brothers Thomas and John Ryan were of Irish descent. They arrived in 1865, and Thomas got caught up in gold fever. He made a fortune for those days when he sold his claim for £3000. Although almost illiterate, he sent his nephew Darby to art school in Paris.

The Way We Were

This portrait, taken on Great Barrier Island, shows a noticeable informality, either because they were close family or on holiday. One gentleman's nautical cap indicates this party may have been holidaying with relatives. The distant island of the Gulf was reached by coastal trading ship, although some pleasure boats may also have visited.

Early life on remote Great Barrier Island, 50 nautical miles and four or five hours by boat from Auckland, was by necessity self-contained. The islanders, with no doctor to call on, dealt with the dramas and passages of life and death themselves. The interrelated pioneering Flinn and Bush families and the Warren and Leroy families still use burial plots on Coine Island, known as Grave Island, off Port Fitzroy, shown in this photograph around 1918.
Members of the Blackwell and Johnson families erected the first trig station (right) near Tryphena just after the turn of the century.

The Way We Were

The wealth of the Gulf islands, including every metre of timber logged, was transported to major ports by a fleet of working scows, like the magnificent Ngaru, seen here crossing the jagged crest of Rangitoto Island. These flat-bottomed craft, designed for the Gulf's tidal estuaries, were brought up on th tide and loaded from wagons when left high and dry. Notice how deeply the Ngaru, bound for St Mary's Bay, is loaded with kauri. The scows remai buoyant even with decks awash. This impressive photograph even shows the detail of the anchor on chains ready to drop.

William Flinn settled in 1836 to work for the Great Barrier Mining Company and was allotted land. This stern-faced group, photographed in front of the Flinn home "Sunnyside" at Port Fitzroy, are celebrating William and Charlotte Flinn's golden wedding anniversary in January 1904. A lifebuoy recovered from the wreck of the SS Wairarapa, wrecked on remote Miner's Head in 1894 with the loss of 135 lives, hangs on the wall beside the front door. The farm was sold in the 1950s and the farmhouse burned down around 1960.

The Way We Were

Kauri Timber Company slipway at Whangaparapara Harbour, Great Barrier Island, showing massive logs as well as sawn planks, to the right. Logging continued on Great Barrier until 1941, when the company closed its plant at Whangaparapara.

Edwardian sightseers pose beside tramlines on the wharf at Whangaparapara, Great Barrier Island. The kauri was dragged out of the rugged bush using bullock teams, tramways, and viaducts or released with floodwater from dams high in the hills to float down to sea.

Hauraki Gulf

In July 1919, Charlotte Agnes Bush married Peter Herbert James Flinn, 20 years her senior, at Port Fitzroy, Great Barrier Island, uniting two pioneer families. The younger man seated to the left is Charlotte's brother Robert Bush.

Boats of all descriptions provided essential links with the mainland for supplies, commerce, communication and leisure. The launching of the Gretchen in 1913 in Auckland was an occasion for best dress. This marvellously detailed photograph was taken from a glass-plate negative.

The Way We Were

The Lillian used to carry bales of wool and other goods from the Duder farm, beyond Maraetai, to Auckland, sailed by the daughter of the house, Emma Duder. This photograph of the Lillian about to pass North Head was taken about 1900.

Baroona, one of the most famous ships of the Gulf, as a working fishing boat. Baroona is thought to have been built in 1904 in New South Wales for an Australian runholder and named after his station. She arrived at the Kaipara Harbour a year later. In 1915 Sanford's converted her into a steam trawler, fishing the Gulf and Bay of Plenty until 1928. She was rebuilt as a double-deck ferry in 1934 and served gallantly for 54 years on the Waiheke run.

Hauraki Gulf

On Auckland Anniversary Day for over 100 years the Waitemata Harbour has hosted one of the biggest regattas in the world, a spectacular sight with the harbour transformed into a sea of sails. This picture shows the regatta flagship some time between 1900 and 1912.

For generations of Aucklanders, the Gulf has been a relatively safe and beautiful place for boating. The dapper, bowler-hatted gentlemen on the launch A.K. 525 are sailing between Auckland and Great Barrier Island.

The Way We Were

This set of delightful photographs, taken between 1913 and 1916 on glass-plate negatives, shows playtime in the Gulf and the increasing independence of women. Above: the picnic ashore was part of the day's cruising, and dressing for it part of the fun. Clara Buchanan (left) wears veils for protection from sun, wind and insects. Left: a game of cricket while ashore added to the fun, with makeshift wickets and a hat used as bails. The women are actively competing. Opposite, top right and bottom: others stripped down to enjoy swimming, the children at North Harbour, Kawau Island. Opposite, top left: the more athletic tried aquaplaning behind a launch, probably like the slender cruiser seen behind this woman skier.

Hauraki Gulf

In a couple of days, the sail from Auckland to Kawau Island provides an enormous range of sights and experiences, with the mainland providing shelter from south-westerlies and plenty of bays and coves to duck into away from weather from the north and east. Annually since the 1920s, Royal New Zealand Yacht Squadron keelers race up from Auckland on Friday night then race again on Saturday at Kawau. The squadron flagship is moored at Mansion House Bay.

Manganese and copper mining began on Kawau Island with colonial government in 1840 and ended in the 1860s with miners moving on to Great Barrier Island. In this glass-plate negative photograph of about 1916, two women, with Clara Buchanan on left, visit the Gothic ruins of the smelting house, with their yacht Gretchen in the background.

Sir George Grey, New Zealand's colonial Governor, bought Kawau Island in 1862, and established his exotic gardens and menagerie. In this glass-plate photograph, taken about 1916, another grand residence can be seen to the left of Mansion House. A large steamer moored at the wharf has brought one of the day picnic excursions so popular at that time. Coastal vessels were used in the off-season for more distant destinations such as Kawau, Great Barrier and Waiheke Islands.

Mansion House, Kawau Island, around 1916. Electric light and power lines have been installed, although the residence is showing some signs of neglect. The original plain-fronted manager's house can be seen in the right wing.

Waiheke Island was promoted early as a holiday resort, and a number of boarding houses were built close to wharves for casual holidaymakers. From the 1890s until the 1920s, the Pegler family farmed and managed the summer boarding house at Pegler's Bay, later named Orapiu.

This photograph, taken around 1914, shows John Pegler with Ellen at centre and seven of the nine Pegler children (the woman with the plait is the photographer's wife).

From Labour Weekend to Easter, life revolved around the operation of the guest house. Mary (far right) was cook and from his teens Selwyn (seated right with rabbit) ran the launch.

The Orapiu property was leased from the McIntoshes, who built a guest house used by well-to-do Aucklanders. Accommodation expanded with a new boarding house as well as the original cottage and four tents. On the far right a double-deck ferry can be seen on dry sand waiting for the tide.

Before the wharf was built, John Pegler rowed out to meet the Northern Steamship Company vessel to collect goods and passengers. This photo was taken in 1918, soon after the completion of the wharf which provided services for the populated end of the island.

The steamship berthed at Pegler's Bay around 1919 is probably the Hauiti, which regularly ran Waiheke excursions. The bay was renamed Orapiu, possibly to avoid confusion with the other bay where Peglers lived. Ellen Pegler was the daughter of Waiheke pioneers Martin and Mary Ann Day. She and her sister married two brothers, and they all remained on Waiheke, the George Peglers farming at Omaru Bay.

Motutapu Island, February 1902. In the sweltering humidity of summer's hottest month, these Edwardians are buttoned up to the neck and wearing boots and petticoats. This charming and elegant group appears relaxed and happy, but an enormous amount of work went into a picnic outing, from the washing, starching and ironing of clothes, to the preparation of lunch and lugging ashore of tent and table.

Heading off for a picnic, Ostend, Waiheke Island, December 1921, in possibly the first motor car on Waiheke, which appeared that year and was used to drive prospective buyers to visit distant sections up for sale.

William and Sarah Brown with John, one of their six sons, photographed around 1910 at their Surfdale homestead. William's parents went to Waiheke Island in the 1850s, his father working as a trader with his schooner Ann. Sarah's parents were the Hodgsons of Omiha, who arrived at Waiheke Island in the 1840s. William grew up on Waiheke without schooling and was illiterate but fluent in Maori. Sarah, however, was very much a lady, and the Brown household employed a tutor and became a part-time school.

A surprise visit in the 1920s from a member of the Walsh Brothers Flying School, who arrived in the biplane at Awaawaroa, in Boarding House Bay. The pilot's wife stayed on at the guesthouse and the pilot dropped mail and returned to town with seafood.

Handsome Edward Brown, pictured with his beautiful wife Katherine around 1910 at Surfdale, built a holiday home at Onetangi but, like his brothers, worked as a mariner. He was a senior captain for the Northern Steamship Company.

The popular paddle-steamer Wakatere plied the Thames-Auckland run for 20 years and was the Northern Steamship Company's chief excursion steamer. Surfdale Wharf, seen here with a lady in typical twenties dress, was opened in 1922 by a party of dignitaries who arrived on the Wakatere and declared that the island would soon have a service every hour, not every three days. The wharf was demolished in 1963.

The homestead at Arran Bay was the home of Andrew and Mary Croll, who married in Scotland without the blessings of her well-to-do parents and emigrated to escape poverty. They were ill-equipped for pioneer farming life at Mercury Island. She knew nothing about housekeeping and preferred to paint, and he was a talented photographer. When that venture failed, they went to Waiheke Island and lived happily at Arran Bay.

The remains of the barque Rewa lie at Moturekareka, one of a string of little islands south of Kawau. The four-masted Rewa was built in 1889 as Alice A. Leigh, the biggest sailing ship ever built by the Whitehaven Shipbuilding Company. Never a fast sailer, she was converted to a barque in 1901. This superb photo, printed from a glass negative, was taken at Moturekareka with the Auckland Harbour Board steam tug Te Awhina in April 1931, the day after towing from Auckland. The owner of both ship and island was Charlie Hansen.

Hauraki Gulf

Life in the Gulf in the 1920s and 1930s spanned two extremes — work and leisure. Farming children started their days early, helping at the cowshed, and often milking again if they got home from school early enough. Alsace Brown (11) in 1931, however, is lucky enough to be milking only the house cow.

A thousand years ago a massive eruption created the Rangitoto Island volcanic cone, which continued to spew lava and ash for the next 700 years. Plant life became established only over the past 200 years. Day excursions to climb the black scoria paths to the summit, like this one in the 1920s, have always been popular.

The girls pictured at a tiny island school range from tiny tots to pre-teens and look strong, healthy and happy.

In the 1920s a formal standard of dress still prevailed. The picnickers, dressed in overcoats and hats, were presided over by Mrs Tercel Senior with daughter Kathleen on her right and daughter-in-law Rita. They brought leather suitcases and wrapped food in brown paper.

At the turn of the century, 150 people lived at Waiheke. Thirty years later there were approximately 500 permanent residents. In this delightful photograph of orderly Ostend in the 1930s, subdivision is well underway. The Ostend Hall can be seen upper left.

Waiheke was THE place for racy young weekenders from Auckland. The highlight of the trip was the lively Saturday night dance held at the different community halls. Richard Towers' crowd came from the Ponsonby-Grey Lynn area in Auckland. The weekend always finished with a ceremonial burying of the dunny, here with the last rites read by one of the gang. The dunny was a source of wierd humour on Waiheke until the islanders got septic tanks.

Richard Towers, a cheerful bachelor in the late 1930s, rolling a smoke in front of the bach at Hekerua Bay, Waiheke, which is between Palm Beach and Oneroa. The last leg of the trip was an hour's walk from the Surfdale Wharf, and even today there is no road to Hekerua Bay.

The Morrisons were a Palm Beach family who bought two sections in the first subdivision in 1922 of Captain Kennedy's land. They managed hotels, and after each two-year stint were able to spend three or four months living at Palm Beach. This photograph shows Winnie Morrison, in the mid-twenties, perhaps waiting for the bus on the road which ran between their home and a boarding house, Simkin House.

The Way We Were

Stylish in 1920s bathers and cloche cap, May Woods was an elocution teacher. The Woods family had a bach at the bottom of what is now Ladd Road at Anzac Bay.

Waiheke Island flapper Lola Lawson, outside the Morrisons' little tin bach at Palm Beach Road, 1928-30. This is where the road now runs in front of a backpackers' hostel, formerly Simkin House. For a while Simkin House was taken over by the Anglican church as a church holiday place. It had originally been shipped in by barge, and is remembered for its wonderful fruit trees, which were raided by neighbourhood children.

Holidaymakers at Waiheke Island who did not own baches could either camp, (like the family above, 1920s-style) or stay in a range of accommodation built around the island's wharves, from cabins to magnificent private hotels. Pictured are the Onetangi Private Hotel (right), taken around 1930, and the Gordon family boarding house at Awaawaroa Bay (top right). Here Jane Gordon (on right) is seen in the front garden during the 1920s.

For 26 years Cecil Brown ran transport around Waiheke Island, including taxis, buses and freight carrying. He was called on in all sorts of emergencies, and his Chevrolet truck doubled as an ambulance, taking patients to the nearest wharf for the rescue dash to hospital in Auckland. He ran the first school bus service too, driving pupils in his Model A Ford. Cecil Brown is pictured centre with his bus fleet in the 1930s.

By the 1920s a network of roads and a public transport system on Waiheke started to link the numerous wharves and the bays previously only reached by boat. The old Palm Beach Store (taken around 1930) was owned by Mr H. Hunter, a returned serviceman who also owned one of the island's first buses and ran the Blue Bus Service. The young women on board are Aroha Raynor and Lola Lawson.

Cecil Brown's truck picking up holidaymakers at Onetangi to take them to the wharf for the trip back to Auckland.

Residential New Zealand life was established on Waiheke Island in the 1930s, and true to every other community, the returned servicemen paraded to commemorate Anzac Day at Ostend Road.

From the earliest days in New Zealand, organised sport followed hard on the heels of settlement. Like every community in the country, Waiheke Islanders loved rugby too, and this 1932 photograph of the Surfdale and Ostend rugby teams shows what kind of grounds they played on. Goalposts were put up on the flat between Ostend and Onetangi.

Waiheke Island rugby team, 1930–1932.

Development on remote Great Barrier Island, which even today has a world-of-its-own appeal for those searching for a place to step out of the rat race, was much slower than on Waiheke Island. During the Great Depression in 1932, relief workers built the Shoal Bay Road, given only pickaxes, shovels, wooden wheelbarrows with iron wheels and tall iron crowbars to prise out boulders and cut the cliffs.

This steam engine, a weighty problem when it was first shipped to Great Barrier Island by barge, was obviously no longer in use at Whangaparapara in 1939.

Hauraki Gulf

The future Air Vice-Marshal Isitt was pilot of the Saro "Cutty Sark" flying boat on loan from the RAF, seen here moored at Shoal Bay, Tryphena, in 1935. The purpose of the visit was to bring a bigwig from the Ministry of Works to find a site for a land airfield, later built at Kaitoke. Sir Leonard Isitt was New Zealand's official signatory of the Japanese surrender to allied forces aboard the American battleship USS Missouri in Tokyo Bay.

Construction of the Claris airfield at Kaitoke, Great Barrier Island, in 1938, was marred by the death of the chief engineer, Bill Claris, whom the airfield was then named after.

Family gathering at Port Fitzroy, Great Barrier Island. Family snapshots are taken at leisure, but leave us wondering what else was happening that day and in these people's hard-working lives. The photograph tells of simpler days when people made their own entertainment.

Great Barrier Island's first wharf at Tryphena was not built until 1934. Pictured at the official opening are five Blackwell brothers, from the pioneer farming family of the district, still represented on the island today. This brought to an end 20 years of bitter wrangling between the communities all vying for the wharf. Unsuccessful in their bid for the wharf, the five Medlands brothers then set about building and financing their own wharf on the other side of the island.

Hauraki Gulf

There was great excitement and everyone turned out to see the first aircraft land on Great Barrier Island at Onerua Bay, now called Red Cliff, at Flinn's Farm in the Port Fitzroy district. The photo was taken for the Auckland Weekly News in 1932.

Once the timber was milled, large areas of Great Barrier Island were farmed by large families like the Flinns at Port Fitzroy, seen here in their best clothes for a family picnic outing. After World War II the decline in coastal shipping and poor planning and policy contributed to the downturn in farming on the island.

In 1928 the Wiltshire was wrecked in fog during a howling gale at the south-eastern end of Great Barrier Island at Rosalie Bay, coming into Auckland from Panama through the Colville Channel. Unlike the other famous Great Barrier wreck, the Wairarapa at the other end of the island, there was no loss of life. Crew tried unsuccessfully to shoot a line ashore from the ship. Finally an heroic seaman called Kehoe from a rescue ship was lowered down 100-metre cliffs in pounding surge and managed to catch the line to bring off the crew.

The Wiltshire hit the cliffs bow on and after a few days broke in half. The stern went into deeper water and the ship was never salvaged. Casks of liquor on board washed up on the eastern beaches and the strict Salvation Army Medlands family were said to have pickaxed open the devil's brew. Other settlers very much liked a drop of top shelf, and spirited the casks away to hide in the bush from police and customs officers.

The Way We Were

"The Gleaners". Flinn family members Charlotte (bending far right), Peter (standing), son Peter and friend Theo Lowe (far left), a shipbuilder from Auckland, gathering oats at the back of the old farmhouse at Port Fitzroy. The oats were tied into sheaves, dried and beaten to get grain to feed the farm's six horses. It was hot, dusty work.

At Flinn's wharf at Port Fitzroy, Great Barrier Island, in the late 1930s, the scow Rahiri waits for the tide to come up and float it alongside the wharf. The planks seen on the wharf were then used as gangplanks to load sheep, which the Rahiri took to stockyards at Leigh. Captain Jock McKinnon, one of the Gulf's most famous skippers, is seen with local farmer Toby Davis and Wag, the Flinns' dog. On remote Great Barrier, the Davis and Flinn families, although farming at quite some distance, worked closely together helping whenever extra hands were needed.

This lovely photograph, taken around 1920, shows the marriage of the well-known skipper Jock McKinnon and Maud (Tiny) Gordon, one of the daughters of the early settler family who ran the farm and boarding house at Awaawarua Bay on Waiheke Island. McKinnon went to sea aged 14, and in 1920 had just started in the Gulf. In 1923, he and a partner salvaged the remains of the wreck of the *Wairarapa* at Great Barrier Island. In 1932 he bought the scow *Rahiri* and worked her around the Gulf for more than 30 years. When he retired the *Rahiri* was the last of the working scows.

The Way We Were

At Cowes on Waiheke Island a narrow wooden pier stretched out into the bay. It was built by the Northern Steamship Company in 1899, regularly used until the mid-1970s and later demolished. This snapshot, of the steamship Wakatere berthed at Cowes, was printed as a postcard.

By the time this photograph of a Great Barrier Island logging camp was taken in the 1930s, most of the accessible big trees had been felled.

There were once about 10 Waiheke Island wharves. The white sand sweep of Onetangi Beach was once interrupted by an Ocean Pier built in 1923 to help market the new subdivision with its "ozone-laden breezes off the wide Pacific". Unfortunately the sea breezes, said to wash the cobwebs from city-weary brains, made the beach too exposed for regular boat services and within 10 years the wharf was disused and breaking up.

Hauraki Gulf

The huge number of passengers packed on board the ferry Condor, perhaps overcrowded by today's standards, gives a good indication of the popularity of "monster excursions" in the 1920s.

In fair weather, sailing around the Gulf's tranquil waters was idyllic. Here, crew members from a yacht have paddled ashore to a secluded spot. The man second left must have swum or been thrown in for a dip because he is dripping wet.

The Way We Were

The yacht Amaryllis is accompanied as it leaves Auckland's Waitemata Harbour in April 1922, en route to England to complete a round-the-world voyage. Patched canvas sail indicates the vulnerability of the yacht on a rare and risky endeavour in days without radio, insurance or safety equipment on board. Long-distance sailors took their lives into their own hands, and in trouble, the Amaryllis was well and truly on its own.

Hauraki Gulf

Wartime in the Gulf. The second intake of navy volunteers were in training on Motuihi Island in July 1941. Naval ratings are shown assembled before going on mid-term leave. Some of the buildings (right) were part of an old quarantine station. Trainees included seamen, stokers, writers (clerical assistants), supply assistants and cooks. They dubbed the navy craft which took them home on leave the "Liberty boat" (top right). It later became the Waitakere ferry, Onewa. Wartime security meant boats were not referred to by real names.

These wartime snaps show military personnel at leisure. During the war Rangitoto, Motutapu, Brown's and Motuihi Islands were off limits, and a boom defence – in effect a gate – was built from Bastion Point to North Head. The Navy controlled all harbour traffic, and civilian boats, including ferries, had to run during daylight regardless of tides. The old tin tub and a pot of boiled water was the only way for naval trainee Royan Bree to bathe on Mokohinau Island.

New dormitories and other buildings were built at the naval station HMS Tamaki on Motuihi Island by public works men.

On Great Barrier Island, Peter Flinn, of the Port Fitzroy family, poses in his Home Guard uniform.

Young Peter Flinn, aged 14, in nautical peaked cap and umbrella on the family farm with Wag the dog.

The Way We Were

At one stage up to 700 army men were stationed on the Great Barrier Island guarding the Claris airfield and the deep-water harbour at Port Fitzroy. Otherwise, the austerity of the war years hardly altered the constant hardship of Great Barrier farming life, especially for women. Charlotte, or Lottie Flinn, however, retains a noticeable serenity and beauty with her dignified older, white-bearded husband Peter, photographed in the late 40s or early 50s with their son Peter and his family.

Hauraki Gulf

Hunting, shooting and fishing — it was a man's world on the Barrier, although in one of these photographs taken during the 1940s a woman is seen on the far right of the hunting party pictured on one of the peaks of the island ranges. Among fishermen, stories abound of the bounty of the ocean and the size of the snapper and crayfish caught in those days.

The Way We Were

Hunters chopping up their quarry with an axe after hunting, Great Barrier Island, late 1940s.

Pig hunters on Great Barrier Island in the 1940s or 1950s pose in front of the remains of the old stamper battery at White Cliffs on the way to Whangaparapara, where gold was discovered in 1892. The very minor gold rush had petered out by 1910, but in its heyday the mining village of over 100 people had its own butchery and bakery.

Hauraki Gulf

The rugged contours of Great Barrier Island, which lies like an ancient tuatara guarding the Hauraki Gulf. Many places are still accessible only by boat, and small craft were an essential part of farming life on the Barrier.

For holidaymakers and for resident families, there was not much in the way of entertainment on offer except what you came up with yourself. Picnics are a recurring and constant theme in the life of the Hauraki Gulf, idyllic glimpses of special moments in simpler days gone by, like this one on Great Barrier Island in the 1940s.

For nearly 40 years Great Barrier children learned their lessons at one of the island's schools, the Whangaparapara Mill School, open from 1906 to 1940. The Kauri Timber Company mill employed many of the parents of these children. The photograph with the sign asking for care and respect in the preservation of the building was taken in January 1981, and shows how the historic building had deteriorated. The building was demolished not long afterwards.

Gannetries dot the rocky promontories of the Hauraki Gulf, like this one at Great Barrier Island. This obliging bird is very much alive as these three intruders measure its wingspan.

Kauri milling was almost over, but the two massive dams on the Kaiarara Creek, Great Barrier Island, were built to last and were still in use in the late 1940s. Today they are only a little the worse for wear and subject to conservation plans to stop further rotting. Timbers are already missing on the wall at top left in this photo.

The Hauraki Gulf, the playground of Auckland, has hosted generations of picnickers on Motuihi Island. The white hats of sailors bob among the crowd of navy families at the Calliope Dockyard picnic in 1947; and members of the Royal New Zealand Yacht Squadron fiercely compete in the annual tug-of-war.

A farewell visit to Great Barrier Island by Governor-General Lord Freyberg, VC, 10 January, 1950. The vice-regal party is departing Tryphena on a naval launch manned by army personnel.

The distinctive cone of Rangitoto Island was built up from layers of ash and volcanic rock, and the island's baches are built on top of volcanic scoria. There will be no more private dwellings built on the protected island and many of the rough old shacks have been dismantled.

The easy lie of Rangitoto Island, connected by a narrow causeway to Motutapu Island, and the many secluded anchorages made it a perfect choice for these boaties in 1946, lazing away an idle hour or two in the sun on top of their cabin cruiser.

For generations of travellers, the Hauraki Gulf begins with embarkation at one of the Auckland wharves. In 1939 the ailing Northern Steamship Company pulled out of the Waiheke run, and by the end of the war three companies were dividing the passenger transport trade. The Devonport Steamship Company bought the former Wellington ferry Muritai, seen at Kings Wharf. A twin-screw steamship, Muritai had been used by the Navy as a minesweeper during the war, but as a passenger boat she was an economic liability.

Hauraki Gulf

Waiheke Island was one of the few Gulf retreats from which it was possible to commute to Auckland. The twin-screw motor vessel Motunui, seen at Kings Wharf, was the main boat taking workers to town, leaving Ostend at 6.20am weekdays and returning to Waiheke from the downtown Ferry Buildings at 5.20pm.

The coal-burning steamship Tangaroa, alongside Kings Wharf, Auckland, was built in 1899 and was still in service in 1953 when this car was photographed being loaded for transport to Waiheke Island. The slow old workhorse Tangaroa was never a popular ship and was scrapped that year. Everything the Waiheke Islanders needed had to be brought in by boats like Tangaroa which, during her run, had carried livestock, cargo, and fresh milk as well as passengers.

The Peregrine, built in Auckland in 1912, started her 47-year career on the harbour crossing to Devonport, but was also used for excursions such as this one around the harbour to Pine Island, Motutapu and Waiheke. The opening of the Harbour Bridge in 1959 spelled the end of the working life of Peregrine and many of her sister ships, and she deteriorated until being broken up in 1981. The double-deck wooden steamship carried nearly 1400 passengers and crew.

The lighthouse on the steep rise of Mokohinau Island, one of an isolated group of islands marking the northern approach to the Hauraki Gulf. It was chosen as a suitable site after the wreck of the brig Caroline close by in 1869. Along with Cuvier and Tiritiri Matangi, it was one of the Gulf's three manned lighthouses. The three lighthouse keepers' cottages were built halfway up the hill, and in 1940-41 a naval radar station was built beside the lighthouse.

Hauraki Gulf

Taking advantage of a visit by the naval ship Belona in the 1950s to Port Fitzroy on Great Barrier Island, a pioneering farming family have their twins christened by the ship's chaplain. The isolation of island life was such that there was no resident clergyman or doctor, and a nurse was in residence on the island only after World War II.

The Way We Were

Way out on its own southeast of Kawau Island, this marker on Flat Rock warned of potential danger to shipping. It is a low-lying rock surrounded by rich fishing grounds, and its light warns larger vessels to give it a wide berth to the east.

Aviation transformed life on the Gulf, providing speed and flexibility and a safety net in times of trouble and emergency. The name of one pilot in particular, Captain Fred Ladd, will always be remembered. He was awarded the MBE in 1963 for services to the people of the Gulf. His Tourist Air Travel began a regular Gulf service in 1954 with one Widgeon aircraft which island-hopped between isolated communities of fishermen and farmers like this one, delivering mail, newspapers, news and good cheer, as well as taking joyriders out for a spin on weekends and women in labour off to hospital.

Hauraki Gulf

The wreck of the barque Rewa was a dramatic sight at Moturekareka Island, south of Kawau Island.

The Albatross, around 1949, punching its way through filthy weather in what looks like a 35-knot southwesterly gale. Notice there is nobody on deck out front. The spray would have gone as high as the smokestack.

The Way We Were

Bill Ward managed the Motuihi Island farm for the Auckland City Council from 1948 to 1951, although ownership was later transferred to the government. He ran about 1200 breeding ewes and a herd of Aberdeen Angus beef cattle. Mustering was done on horseback in the early 1950s by Bill and his son Jim (mounted).

The scow Rahiri and crusty Captain Jock McKinnon provided transport of stock and farm gear for farmer Bill Ward on Motuihi. The scow is tied alongside the farm jetty awaiting cattle. Bill and his wife loved the island and lived there until he died suddenly of a coronary aged 53 years.

Hauraki Gulf

As recently as 1956, a whaling station was in operation on Great Barrier Island at Whangaparapara. The enterprise, however, was short-lived and unlucky. These photos show whale carcasses being towed to the remote station where they were cut up by huge cross-saws on the flensing floor and the blubber removed. Huge vats and a boiler house replaced the trypots of olden-day whaling.

The two whalers standing on the flensing floor show just how massive the whale is.

Humorous today, these two sporting chaps with greased-back hair and racing cap are out for a spin in the newest, smoothest runabout of the 1950s, complete with steering wheel.

The passing of an era. At Cowes Bay, Waiheke Island, in 1957, the private hotel is abandoned, a shadow of its former glory when the bay and hotel were a social Mecca and hosted the annual Waiheke regatta. Thousands of city visitors in their finery arrived on the paddle steamer Wakatere, decked out with flags and with a brass band playing. The guest-house, as the sign in the photo says, also provided post office, store, dancing, and fishing (fires prohibited). It was owned by Innes Parres, who as a 13-year-old Portuguese sailor jumped ship at Waiheke Island. The old house was finally destroyed by fire.

PALM BEACH
4-SQUARE STORE
ALL ABOUT PALM BEACH

If you walk along the Palm Beach shore
   A-lookin' and a-viewin',
If you ask some young wench, "What's the score?"
   She won't say "Nothin' doin'."
There's always something going on,
   Just started or completed;
Though many folk there are retired,
   They've not retired defeated.

They go dancing old and new time
   In the Community Hall,
And they play at indoor bowling —
   "Come on, baby, roll that ball."
They play cards and worship (Sundays)
   In the little Domain Hall:
There the roaring Buffaloes gather —
   See their horns upon the wall.

You can hire a boat or surfboard
   Where the waves come tumbling in;
Fish for schnapper or for kingfish
   With rod, line or just bent pin.
Ride the "Widgie" up to Auckland —
   Airport's just two miles away;
Or, for just a little extra, have it
   Land you in the bay.

Take a boat trip "down the Island",
   Leave Ostend for further ports —
Only costs you a few shillings —
   Back same afternoon of course.
Ride on bus or take a taxi
   Sightseeing the Island bays;
Join a library, go in swimming,
   Sunbathe on the beach and laze.
Palm Beach once was "Whakarite" —
   Here the Maori fought and fed,
Feasted on the luckless prisoners —
   On the ones that were real dead.

"Fifteen miles from Auckland town, Catch a boat and come on down, For holidays or place to live, Palm Beach has the most to give." The rhyming verse is by Gordon Ingham, who published Waiheke Island's newspaper for many years.

THIS IS
PALM BEACH
Waiheke Island

Fifteen miles from Auckland town,
Catch a boat and come on down —
For holidays or place to live,
Palm Beach has the most to give.

Ingham's talents and sense of humour came out again in typical '50s style with this fun map caricaturing businesses and residents of the island.

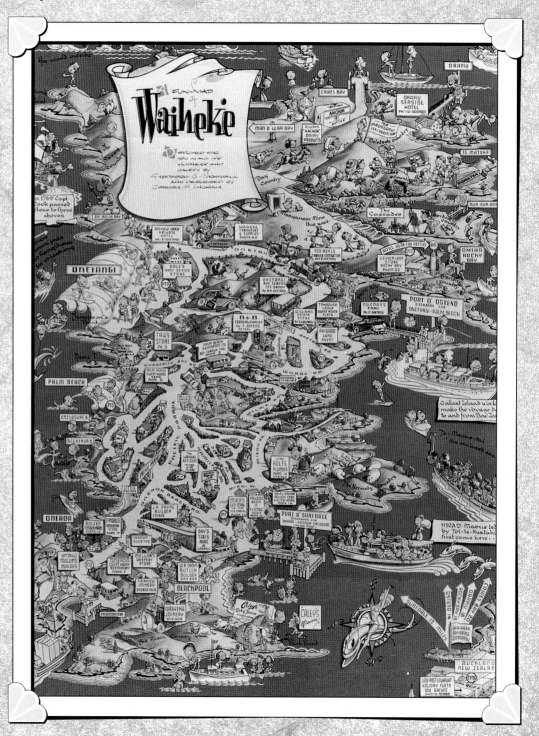

The march of progress on Waiheke Island. Electricity arrives in 1953, and the historic erection of the first power pole is recorded. The power board service truck advertises "progress and development".

In spite of the tranquillity in this view of Orapiu Bay, parts of Waiheke were fast becoming satellite suburbs of Auckland.

The Way We Were

Part of the wartime defence network of the Hauraki Gulf were gun emplacements and tunnels at Stony Batter on the far eastern end of Waiheke Island. This fascinating series of photographs shows Number One gun completed (two soldiers leaning on it) and the arrival of Number Two gun in parts. Building the crane was an engineering job in itself.

Camp accommodation was pretty basic at Stony Batter. The group beside the jeep are at the orderly's hut.

Soldiers about to complete the task of swinging the gun into place pose with Lieutenant Harvey.

The Way We Were

Cars parked outside the popular Captain's Table Tearooms at Palm Beach. At the domain in the background a pipe band can just be seen marching with a big bass drum. The hall was originally a St John Ambulance hut and was later enlarged. It was demolished in the 1980s.

The Waiheke Island volunteer fire brigade.

Hauraki Gulf

A common sight wherever you are in the Gulf are the gannets. Mr Stein Senior (right) became a world authority on gannets, which he ringed in order to trace at Gannet Rock, Waiheke, around 1955.

Captain Fred Ladd, the daring aviator of the Gulf, took winners of a Waiheke Island high school essay competition on the inaugural Auckland-Waiheke flight in 1956. His most daring exploit was to fly illegally under the Harbour Bridge.

Waiheke Island continued to host the daredevil TT motorbike races at Ostend through the 1940s and 1950s. Spectators can be seen halfway up the hill lining the dirt road, awaiting the speeding contestant number 11. Contestant number 17, Len Perry, in leather pants and jacket with goggles, rides into the new decade on a Vincent motorcycle.

The ones we don't see many of now. Farley Scott at the family beach at Man O'War Bay, Waiheke Island, in the 1950s with a fish that truly lived up to the stories.

The Way We Were

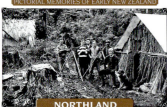
NORTHLAND

WAIKATO

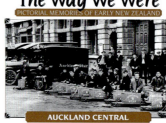
AUCKLAND CENTRAL

DUNEDIN / COASTAL OTAGO

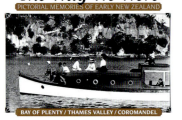
BAY OF PLENTY / THAMES VALLEY / COROMANDEL

WELLINGTON

AUCKLAND – SOUTH & EAST

ROTORUA / TAUPO / CENTRAL NORTH ISLAND

TARANAKI / WANGANUI

NELSON / MARLBOROUGH / WEST COAST

AUCKLAND – NORTH SHORE / WAITAKERE

SOUTHLAND / CENTRAL OTAGO / FIORDLAND

CHRISTCHURCH

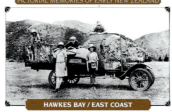
HAWKES BAY / EAST COAST

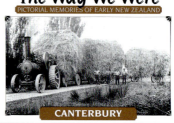
CANTERBURY

MANAWATU / WAIRARAPA

This sixteen-volume series, covering the entire country, was published in 1994. Your local bookseller can order the titles you require or copies may be purchased direct from **The Way We Were**, PO Box 100-749, North Shore Mail Centre, Auckland 1330. Enclose a cheque for $24 per copy (includes postage & packaging). Credit card facility not available.